The Maple Syrup Baking and Dessert Cookbook

by Ken Haedrich

For Evelyn —
Best wishes
Ken Haedrich

With lettering and Illustrations by Ginger Brown

American Impressions Book Company

The Maple Syrup Baking and Dessert Cookbook

Published by American Impressions Book Company
Box 101
Rumney, New Hampshire 03266

ISBN 0-942550-00-5

Table of Contents

Introduction..5

Cookies and Bars

Ben's Black Bottom Cheesecake Bars...............7
Cindy's Coffee Chip Cookies.........................8
Pumpkin or Squash Cookies...........................9
Almond Nirvana.......................................10
Blonde Ginger Cut-Out Cakes.........................11
Baklava..12
Killer Bars..14
GORP Bars..15
Pecan Pie Shortbread.................................16
Whole Wheat Hermits..................................17
Soft Almond Cookies..................................18
Whole Wheat Oat Chews................................19
Rich Short Crust.....................................20

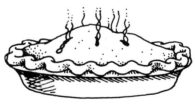

Pies and Pastries

4 Piecrusts..21
Apple Pie, Vermont Style.............................23
Sweet Potato Pie.....................................24
Apple Pan Dowdy......................................25
Blueberry Vanilla Cream Pie..........................26

Cranberry Orange Pie 27
Maple Pecan Pie 28
Apple Pear Pie 29
Viennese Apple Turnovers 30

Breads and Cakes

Golden Cornmeal Cake 32
Minnesota Kate's Cosmic Carrot Cake 33
Wheat Germ Applesauce Muffins 34
Zucchini Bread (with Chinese influences) 35
Sour Cream Tea Bread 36
Cinnamon Sticky Buns 37
Better-Than-The-Monks' Fruitcake 38

Puddings, Ice Cream, and other Goodies

Woodstock Inn Frozen Maple Souffle 40
Maple Graham Crackers 41
Indian Pudding 42
Cinnamon Nut Swirl (Ice Cream) 43
Baked Custard 44
Blueberry Grunt 45
A Gallon of Granola 46

Introduction

When the idea for this book first surfaced a while back, I had mixed feelings about actually taking up the project. On the one hand, baking with maple syrup has always been one of my special passions; having worked as a professional chef in various parts of New England, I reach for it almost instinctively when I'm developing new recipes.

On the other hand, I had to ask: given the cost of maple syrup, would there be sufficient interest among the baking public for such a collection?

I took my concerns to the streets. I spoke to home cooks as well as professional cooks and asked them what they thought. I talked to producers of syrup and bookstore owners, too. I asked for their opinions, told them of my plans, sought their advice.

What I learned from this grassroots marketing research allayed any trepidations I may have had. Indeed, almost everyone I spoke to encouraged me to write this book. New England cooks do bake with maple syrup, I found out — maybe not every day or even every week, but often enough to warrant a short book of reliable, easy-to-follow and irresistably good recipes.

On these counts I hope I have succeeded. I also hope you find will these recipes to your liking and that you'll return to these pages often.

Ken Haedrich

Some Pointers

* Please observe notes about temperatures of ingredients. Doing so will prevent congealing and other mishaps.

* For baking purposes, buy dark amber syrup. It is the least expensive grade, with the richest maple flavor.

* Buy your syrup locally; support your neighbors who produce the stuff. By all means don't order your syrup from one of these lease-a-maple-tree outfits that advertise in magazines. They charge a lot, deliver little.

* If you do live within the maple syrup region, check with your state extension service for a list of producers near you.

This book is dedicated
to my main squeeze, Karen,
and to our two little squeezes,
Ben and Tess.

Ben's Black Bottom Cheesecake Bars

This is the sort of cheesecake I make most often; because it is thinner than a smaller, round cake it cools more much quickly and can be eaten the same day.

1 recipe Rich Short Crust (page 20)

1 lb. cream cheese, softened.
½ cup sour cream, room temp.
2 eggs, room temp.
3/4 cup maple syrup, room temp.
1 teaspoon vanilla
1 teaspoon lemon juice
1-2 cups chocolate chips

Prepare the crust. and line a 9"x13" glass baking dish with it. Refrigerate while you make the cheesey stuff.

Preheat oven to 425°.

With an electric mixer, beat the cream cheese and sour cream until fluffy. Add eggs, one at a time. Slowly drizzle in the maple syrup, followed by the vanilla and lemon juice.

Sprinkle the chocolate chips evenly over the crust. Gently pour on the cheese mixture. Bake at 425° for 15 minutes, then lower heat to 350° and bake another 30 minutes. The cake will have puffed nicely (it will fall) and developed cracks across the top. Cool and chill before cutting. 2 dozen bars.

Mint Chip Cheesecake: add <u>one</u> drop of mint oil to the cheese mixture.

Cindy's Coffee Chip Cookies

This recipe is dedicated to my friend Cindy, who'll take her coffee any way she can get it.

> 1 cup softened, unsalted butter
> 1 cup maple syrup, room temp.
> 1½ tablespoons instant coffee
> 2 tablespoons hot water
> 2 teaspoons vanilla or almond extract
> 1½ cups whole wheat flour
> 1 cup unbleached flour
> 2 cups finely chopped walnuts (either
>   blenderize or food process them)
> 1 teaspoon baking soda
> ½ teaspoon salt
> 1½ cups chocolate chips

Preheat oven to 350°.

Cream butter with an electric mixer. Continue to beat while you drizzle in the maple syrup, coffee dissolved in hot water, and the vanilla or almond extract.

In a separate bowl, toss together the flours, walnuts, salt and soda. Beat into the creamed mixture, adding about a cup at a time; beat until smooth. Fold in chips. Let batter sit 15 minutes.

Drop heaping tablespoons of batter onto a greased cookie sheet, leaving about 2" between the glops.* Bake about 15 minutes, just until the edges begin to brown.
Cool on a rack.

*  = 1 glop.

Pumpkin or Squash Cookies

Here's an unusual treat, packed with the fruits of autumn. It's a very soft cookie, with just the right amount of spice.

> 1 cup maple syrup
> 1 cup cooked pumpkin or squash (cooled)
> 1 egg
> 1 teaspoon vanilla
> ½ cup soft butter
> 1 cup whole wheat flour
> 1 cup unbleached flour
> 1 teaspoon baking soda
> 1 teaspoon baking powder
> ½ teaspoon salt
> ½ teaspoon each: cinnamon & nutmeg
> ½ cup chopped pecans
> 1 cup peeled, grated apple

Preheat oven to 350°.

Put first 4 ingredients in the blender and buzz until smooth. Cream the butter with an electric mixer. Add about half the buzzed mixture.

In a separate bowl, toss together remaining ingredients except pecans and apple. Add half of this to the creamed mixture, stirring just until blended. Stir in the rest of the pumpkin purée, then finally the remaining dry mix. Gently fold in pecans and apples.

Spoon heaping tablespoonsful onto a greased cookie sheet, leaving a couple of inches for spreading. Bake for 15-20 minutes, until the bottom edges are just starting to brown. Makes about 3 dozen.

Almond Nirvana

The ultimate in a cookie bar, these make a super Christmas gift. Warning: if you're counting calories or pennies, these just won't do. Read this recipe through before you make it, to get the hang of the technique.

To make the crust:

2 sticks soft butter
½ cup brown sugar
1 egg (room temp.)

3 cups flour <u>or</u> 2 cups flour and 1 cup almond meal

Cream butter and brown sugar. Beat in the egg. Work in the flour and/or almond meal, ½ cup at a time. You should end up with a not-too-moist but rather soft ball of dough. Divide in half, dust each half with flour then form each into a square about 1" thick. Wrap each half in plastic and refrigerate for an hour.

Preheat oven to 375° when you remove the dough from the fridge. Roll each half into a rectangle approximately 11" x 8". Place the halves, overlapping slightly at the middle seam, on a 10" x 15" jelly roll pan. Gently tuck the dough into the corners and press lightly to seal at the center. Trim the dough flush with the top of the pan. Refrigerate for 10 minutes. Prick the dough several times with a fork, then bake at 375° for 15 minutes. Let cool.

To make the topping:

1 stick butter
¾ cup maple syrup
½ cup brown sugar
¼ cup honey

¼ cup heavy cream
2 cups chopped almonds
1 teaspoon vanilla

Heat butter, syrup, sugar & honey. When the mixture begins to boil add the cream. When it returns to a boil let it boil for 2 minutes. Remove from heat, stir in the almonds and vanilla. Spread this mixture evenly over the crust. (If you have a second jelly roll pan, "double pan" the first one for more even baking. Simply put one inside the other.) Bake for 20 minutes at 375° Cool thoroughly before slicing. About 2 dozen bars. (They won't last.)

Blonde Ginger Cut-Out Cakes

A great recipe for holiday cut-out cookies. This dough has a soft, putty-like texture and is very easy to roll. Give it at least 2 hours in the fridge before rolling.

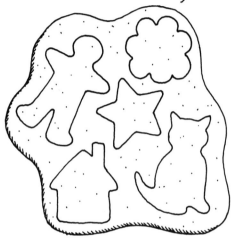

2/3 cup shortening
1/3 cup soft butter
1 cup maple syrup, room temp.
1 tablespoon molasses
1/2 teaspoon vanilla
3 1/2 cups flour (may be part
    whole wheat)
2 teaspoons baking soda
1/2 teaspoon salt
1/2 teaspoon ginger
1/4 teaspoon each: nutmeg and
    cloves

Cream together the shortening and butter. Drizzle in the maple syrup, molasses and vanilla, beating until smooth. Toss together remaining ingredients, adding to the creamed mix about a cup at a time. Chill the dough at least 2 hours.

Preheat oven to 350°.

Roll the dough not quite one quarter inch thick. Cut into whatever shapes you like, either freehand or with cookie cutters. Bake about 10 minutes. Let cool briefly on the baking sheet before transferring to a wire rack.

Baklava

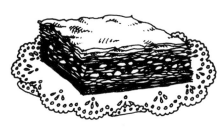

Not particularly authentic, but every bit as good as traditional versions. Best if left to mellow for 24 hours before eating. I suggest reading the phyllo box for tips on working with the phyllo leaves.

First make the syrup:

1 1/2 cups maple syrup
1/4 cup honey
2/3 cup water
1 tablespoon lemon juice

Heat above almost to the boiling point. Turn down heat and let simmer 10 minutes. Allow to cool to room temp.

Now the filling:

4 cups chopped walnuts
1 teaspoon cinnamon and 1/2 teaspoon cloves
grated rind of 1 lemon
1/2 cup warm honey

Combine above in a bowl and set aside. To assemble you'll need: about 14 tablespoons melted, <u>unsalted</u> butter.
24 sheets of phyllo, about 9 1/2" x 13 1/2"

Preheat oven to 350°.

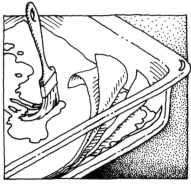

Butter a 9" x 13" baking pan. Lay 12 sheets of phyllo in the pan, buttering each layer with the melted butter.

After the 12 sheets, evenly spread half the filling on top.

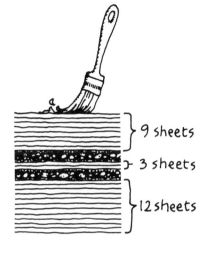

} 9 sheets

} 3 sheets

} 12 sheets

Cover that with 3 more sheets of buttered phyllo, the remaining filling, then the final 9 sheets of buttered phyllo.

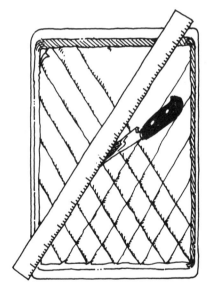

Here's the tricky part. Using a long ruler laid on top of the pan for a guide, cut into diamond shapes about 1" wide —as wide as the ruler, probably.

However, only cut halfway down, leaving the bottom layers intact.

Bake about 1½ hours, until golden brown on top. Remove from the oven and let sit on a rack for 30 minutes. Pour the cooled syrup evenly over the baklava. After it has cooled, finish the cuts.

13

Killer Bars

This is the best of all worlds: the lush gooiness of a pecan pie crowded with chocolate and nuts. All on a rich pastry.

1 recipe Rich Short Crust (Page 20)

2 eggs
1 cup maple syrup
1 teaspoon vanilla
¼ cup flour
½ teaspoon baking powder
1 cup chopped nuts (not peanuts —
    too pedestrian)
1 cup chopped dates
1 cup (at least) chocolate chips
½ - 1 cup grated coconut (optional)

Preheat oven to 425°.

Prepare Rich Short Crust, if you haven't already, and line a 9" x13" pan with it. Chill until you use it.

Beat together the eggs, maple syrup and vanilla. Mix together the flour and powder and sprinkle into the egg mixture while whisking. Fold in the remaining ingredients. Pour into the prepared crust and spread evenly. Bake at 425° for 15 minutes, then reduce heat to 350° and bake about another 15-20 minutes. The crust will be golden and the top lightly golden. Cool before cutting. 2 dozen bars.

Gorp Bars

Good Old Raisin and Peanut bars. Moist and chewy, great for brown baggers.

1 cup peanut butter
½ cup soft butter
1 cup maple syrup
1 egg
1 teaspoon vanilla
½ teaspoon baking soda
1 cup rolled oats
1 cup flour, either white
  or whole wheat
1½ cups finely chopped peanuts
1½ cups raisins

Preheat oven to 350°.

Cream peanut butter and butter with an electric mixer. Slowly add the maple syrup, then the egg, vanilla and baking soda, beating all the while. Stir in the oats and flour, just to blend, followed by the peanuts and raisins. With floured hands, pat the mixture evenly into a greased, 9" x 13" baking pan — I normally use glass. Bake about 30 minutes, until the edges are just beginning to brown. Let cool before cutting.

Pecan Pie Shortbread

A buttery bottom covered with a pecan pie sort of topping. These are quite rich, best cut in small squares and a nice nibbler around the holidays.

For the Shortbread:

> 1 cup soft butter
> ½ cup maple syrup, room temp.
> ½ teaspoon salt (only if using unsalted butter)
> 3 cups flour

With an electric mixer, beat the butter, slowly drizzling in the maple syrup. Add salt and beat in the flour, ½ cup at a time. Work in the last cup of flour using a wooden spoon, otherwise the mix will just bunch up in the beaters. With floured hands, pat the soft dough evenly into a greased 8"x 12" glass baking pan. Refrigerate while you make the topping.

Pecan Pie Topping:

> 1 egg
> ½ cup maple syrup
> 1 teaspoon vanilla
> 4 tablespoons melted butter
> 1 tablespoon white flour
> 1½ cups chopped pecans

Preheat oven to 350°.

With an electric mixer, beat the egg about a minute until light in color and texture. Continue beating, adding maple syrup, vanilla, melted butter and flour. Add nuts. Spread evenly over shortbread and bake about 40 minutes, until topping is set. Cool before cutting.

Whole Wheat Hermits

Hermits are a generally spicy, festive affair, crowded with chopped nuts and fruits and sometimes sweetened with molasses. If you're a molasses fancier, substitute some for an equal portion of maple syrup.

½ cup soft butter
½ cup maple syrup
¼ cup brown sugar
1 egg
1 teaspoon sweet spices: any combination
  of cinnamon, nutmeg, cloves, etc.
1¼ cups whole wheat flour
1 teaspoon baking powder
1 cup raisins
1 cup chopped nuts
½ cup chopped dates, figs or combination
grated rind of 1 orange (optional)
up to 1 cup chocolate chips (for
  chocolate freaks)

Preheat oven to 350°.

Cream butter, syrup and sugar. Beat in the egg. Sift together the dry ingredients and blend into the butter mixture. Add all the remaining ingredients and mix well. Spoon tablespoon globs of batter onto greased cookie sheets. Bake for 15 minutes. The tops will be slightly resistant to finger pressure. Makes about 2½ dozen.

Soft Almond Cookies

I like this recipe as is, but for a fancier cookie press an almond in the middle of the cookie before you bake it.

> 1/2 cup butter, softened
> 3 oz. cream cheese, softened
> 3/4 cup maple syrup, room temp.
> 1 egg
> 1 teaspoon almond extract
> 2 teaspoons lemon rind, grated
> 2 cups ground almonds (meal)
> 1 1/2 cups flour
> 1/2 teaspoon salt
> 1 teaspoon baking powder

Preheat oven to 350°

With an electric mixer, cream butter and cream cheese. Continue to beat, adding the maple syrup in a slow drizzle. Then beat in the egg, almond extract and lemon rind.

Toss together remaining ingredients, then add to the liquids, stirring just until all is moistened. Spoon the cookies by the tablespoon onto a lightly greased cookie sheet. Bake about 15 minutes, until the bottoms are golden and the tops just slightly resistant to finger pressure.

Whole Wheat Oat Chews

A very basic and delicious cookie. A real classic.

> 8 tablespoons (1 stick) soft butter
> 1 tablespoon molasses
> 3/4 cup maple syrup
> 1 cup whole wheat flour
> 1 cup rolled oats
> 1/2 teaspoon salt
> 1/2 teaspoon baking soda
> 1/2 teaspoon each: cinnamon and allspice
> 1 cup raisins (optional but recommended)

Preheat oven to 350°.

Cream the butter and molasses with an electric mixer until fluffy. Still beating, slowly drizzle in the maple syrup. Toss together remaining ingredients, including raisins if you're using them, and add to the butter mixture. Beat until blended. Spoon by the heaping tablespoon onto greased baking sheets. Bake 12 - 15 minutes. The tops should still be soft and the edges only barely beginning to brown. Cool on the pan for a few minutes before transferring to wire racks. Makes about 2 dozen.

Oat Crisps: Omit the molasses and substitute white flour for the whole wheat. Add 1 teaspoon vanilla to the creamed mixture and omit the spices and raisins

Rich Short Crust

This is a good, maple-laced, general-purpose cookie bar crust. Very simple to prepare and pat into a 9" x 13" pan. I use it for Killer Bars (p.14) and Ben's Black Bottom Cheesecake Bars. (p.7).

> 3/4 cup unsalted butter, softened
> 1/3 cup maple syrup, room temp.
> 1/2 teaspoon vanilla
> 2 cups unbleached flour
> 1/4 teaspoon salt

Cream the butter with an electric mixer. Drizzle in the maple syrup and vanilla and beat until well blended. Add the remaining flour, 1/3 cup at a time, working it in more gently with a wooden spoon. Pat evenly into a 9" x 13" baking pan; roll with a bottle to even it out.

Refrigerate until needed.

Pies and Pastries

4 Piecrusts
(3 of which have healthy, grainy overtones)

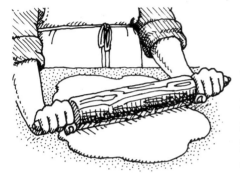

All-American Piecrust

2¼ cups all-purpose flour
½ teaspoon salt
¾ cup vegetable shortening, chilled
2 tablespoons butter
2 teaspoons lemon juice
5-7 tablespoons cold water

Toss flour and salt together in a medium-size bowl. Add vegetable shortening and butter, breaking the fat into smaller chunks with your hands. Using a pastry blender, cut the fat into the flour until the mixture resembles particles of rice. It should not become pasty.

Sprinkle the lemon juice over the crumb mixture followed by 1 tablespoon of cold water. Toss with a fork. Add remaining water, one tablespoon at a time, tossing and mixing with a fork after each addition. When the dough coheres, form it into a ball, divide in half, then flatten each half into a 1" thick disc. Wrap in plastic and refrigerate until needed.

Basic Whole Wheat Crust

1¾ cups whole wheat flour
¾ cup all-purpose flour
½ teaspoon salt
¾ cup vegetable shortening or lard, chilled
¼ cup butter, chilled
2 teaspoons lemon juice
5-7 tablespoons cold water

Toss flours and salt together in a medium-sized bowl. Add the vegetable shortening and butter, breaking them into chunks with your hands. Using a pastry blender, cut the fat into the flour until the mixture is in small, fairly uniform pieces, ranging in size from rice to small peas. Do not overblend. Sprinkle lemon juice and 1 tablespoon water

21

over the crumb mixture, tossing it with a fork. Add remaining water, sprinkling it on a tablespoon at a time, until dough coheres into a ball when packed. Divide the dough in half, flatten each half into a 1" thick disc, wrap in plastic and refrigerate until needed.

Oatmeal Crust

1¼ cups rolled oats, finely ground in blender
3/4 cup all-purpose flour
1/2 cup whole wheat flour
1/2 teaspoon salt

3/4 cup vegetable shortening, chilled
2 tablespoons butter, chilled
3-4 tablespoons cold water

Toss flours and salt together in a medium-sized bowl. Add the vegetable shortening and butter, breaking the fat into smaller pieces with your hands. Cut the fat into the flour with a pastry blender, until the mixture is in small pieces about the size of baby peas. Sprinkle on the water, a tablespoon at a time, until the dough packs easily into a ball. Divide the dough in half, wrap in plastic and refrigerate until needed.

Note: Due to the fragile nature of this dough, I don't recommend attempting a lattice with it.

Sesame Corn Crust

1 cup all-purpose flour
3/4 cup cornmeal
1/2 cup whole wheat flour
1/4 cup toasted sesame seeds, cooled
1/2 teaspoon salt

3/4 cup vegetable shortening, chilled
2 tablespoons butter, chilled
4-5 tablespoons cold water

Toss together first five ingredients in a medium-sized bowl. Add the vegetable shortening and butter, breaking it into smaller pieces with your hands. Using a pastry blender, cut the fat into the flour until the mixture is in small pieces about the size of rice and tiny peas. Do not overmix. Sprinkle the water over the crumb mixture a tablespoon at a time, tossing with a fork. When the dough coheres, pack into a ball, divide and form into 1" thick discs. Wrap the discs in plastic and refrigerate until needed.

Note: Due to the crumbly nature of this dough, I don't recommend it for lattice crusts.

The high proportion of pies in this book should give you some idea how crazy I am about them. Creating new piecrusts,  especially grainy ones, I find particularly exciting. Try your hand at some of the preceding crusts ~ they can be used interchangeably with the following collection of pies.

Apple Pie, Vermont Style

Some people like a slice of cheddar with their apple pie. Here I put the cheese in the pie. Serve this slightly warm, so the cheese is still soft.

> Pastry for a two-crust pie
>
> 5 cups apples, peeled, cored, and sliced
> ½ cup maple syrup
> ⅓ cup heavy cream
> 2 teaspoons lemon juice
> 1½ tablespoons quick-cooking tapioca
> 1 cup Cheddar cheese, coarsely grated

Preheat oven to 450°.

Combine filling ingredients in the order listed. Pour into an unbaked pie shell. Cover with the top pastry, sealing and crimping the edge. Bake for 20 minutes, then reduce heat to 375° and bake another 35-45 minutes, until bubbly thick.

Sweet Potato Pie

Instead of sweet potato you could use an equal portion of winter squash. The filling is made right in the blender: easy and very little cleanup, especially if you've a frozen crust on hand.

Pastry for a single crust pie

2 cups cooked sweet potatoes
3 eggs
½ cup maple syrup
1 tablespoon molasses
1 cup milk or light cream
¼ teaspoon salt
1 teaspoon each : cinnamon, allspice, ginger

Partially bake the pie crust in a 425° oven for about 10 minutes. Let cool 10 minutes.

Put all the filling ingredients in the blender and purée until smooth. Pour into the pie shell and bake at 425° for 15 minutes. Lower the heat to 350° and bake another half hour, until a sharp knife inserted in the pie emerges clean. The top will puff and split, most likely. Serve at any temperature, with whipped cream or ice cream.

Apple Pan Dowdy

This is one of my favorite desserts of all time. I make it with an oatmeal crust rather than a biscuit topping, which usually sucks up too much of the liquid.

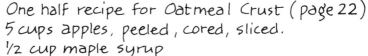

One half recipe for Oatmeal Crust (page 22)
5 cups apples, peeled, cored, sliced.
½ cup maple syrup
2 tablespoons molasses (optional)
1 tablespoon flour
1 teaspoon each: cinnamon and allspice
2 tablespoons butter or cream

Preheat oven to 425°.

Mix first five ingredients. Spread evenly in a buttered 9" x 9" baking pan. Dot with butter or drizzle with cream. Roll crust slightly larger than baking pan. Lay on top of apples, tucking edges in beneath top edge. Pierce the crust a few times with a sharp knife. Bake at 425° for 10 minutes, then lower heat to 350° and bake another 30 minutes. The top should be golden and the insides bubbly. Serve warm, with whipped cream. Makes about 6-8 servings.

Blueberry Vanilla Cream Pie

Try this made with one of my whole grain crusts. Serve with whipped cream or Cinnamon-Nut Swirl Ice Cream (p. 43)

Pastry for a two-crust pie

4 cups blueberries
½ cup maple syrup
¼ cup heavy cream
pinch of cinnamon
grated rind of 1 lemon
2 teaspoons vanilla extract
3½ tablespoons cornstarch

Preheat oven to 450°.

Line a 9" pie pan with the bottom pastry. Refrigerate. Mix together all the filling ingredients except the cornstarch. Sift the cornstarch over the blueberries, a tablespoon at a time, stirring after each. Let sit 10 minutes before filling pie.

Moisten outer rim of bottom pastry with wet fingertips. Lay on the top pastry, pressing lightly to seal where you've moistened. Trim the dough flush with the side of the pan and crimp with the tines of a fork for a tighter seal.

OR... cut the dough with scissors about ½" from the pan's edge, and turn the dough under while forming into an upright ridge:

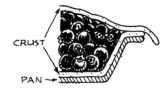

In either case, poke a few steam vents up top. Bake at 450° for 20 minutes, then lower heat to 375° and bake about another 40-45 minutes, until bubbly thick.

Variation: For a less rich version, omit the cream and reduce cornstarch to 3 tablespoons.

Cranberry Orange Pie

A great pie for the holidays. Without question my favorite berry pie.

Pastry for a two-crust pie

5 cups fresh, not canned, cranberries
1 cup maple syrup
1/2 cup brown sugar
1 orange, halved and sections cut out
1 tablespoon finely grated orange rind
1 teaspoon allspice or cloves
1/4 cup raisins
1 1/2 tablespoons quick-cooking tapioca

Preheat oven to 425.°

Line a 9" pie pan with bottom pastry. In a large bowl, stir together all the filling ingredients. Pour into pie shell. Slightly moisten outer rim of bottom crust with water. Lay on the top crust, pressing gently where you've moistened. Trim crust and crimp with a fork for a tightly sealed, decorative edge. Pierce top crust two or three times with a fork — steam vents. Bake at 425° for 20 minutes then lower heat to 375° and bake another 30-40 minutes. Serve warm.

Maple Pecan Pie

Serve with vanilla ice cream or whipped cream.

> 3 eggs
> 1 cup maple syrup
> ½ cup brown sugar
> ½ cup melted butter
> pinch salt
> 1 teaspoon vanilla
> 1 tablespoon flour
> 1 2/3 cup pecan halves

One half of any piecrust recipe (p. 21-22)

Preheat oven to 425°.

With an electric mixer, beat the eggs at high speed for two minutes. Add remaining ingredients (except pecans) in the order listed. Beat another minute. Spread pecans in the unbaked shell then gently pour in the liquid. Bake at 425° for 10 minutes then lower to 375° and bake about another half hour. The pie should be golden, puffed and not soupy in the middle. 8 servings.

Apple Pear Pie

Naturally, you could use all apples here instead of the combination of fruit.

Pastry for a two-crust pie
4 cups apples, peeled, cored and sliced
2 cups pears,   "   "   "
juice and grated rind of 1 lemon
1/2 cup raisins
1/4 cup maple syrup
1/4 cup heavy cream
1 1/2 tablespoons quick cooking tapioca
1 teaspoon cinnamon

Preheat oven to 425°.

Line a 9" pie pan with the bottom pastry. In a large bowl, stir together all the filling ingredients until well blended. Spread evenly in the shell. Moisten the outer rim of the shell with water. Lay on the top crust, pressing lightly where you've moistened. Trim crust with a sharp knife then crimp with a fork. Pierce several air vents in the top crust with your fork. Bake at 425° for 15 minutes, then lower heat to 375° and bake for another 30-40 minutes, until bubbly hot inside. Slice when warm.

29

Viennese Apple Turnovers

These are very easy to make and just right for brown bag lunches. This recipe makes 4 rather large turnovers but you can actually make them any size you like.

The dough:

> 1 cup flour
> ¼ teaspoon salt
> ⅓ cup cream cheese, chilled
> ⅓ cup unsalted butter, chilled
> 2 tablespoons (approx.) cold water

Toss flour and salt. Add butter and cream cheese and cut them into the flour with a pastry blender until all the flour is touched by the butter/cream cheese, but the pieces are still on the large size. Add the water, a tablespoon at a time, balling the dough with your hands. If it fails to cohere, add more cold water, just drops at a time. Flatten the dough into a 1" disc, wrap in plastic and refrigerate for about an hour and start working on...

The filling:

> 1½ cups apples, peeled, cored and chopped
> ½ cups raisins
> ½ cup dates
> ½ teaspoon cinnamon
> ⅓ cup maple syrup

Combine filling ingredients and heat gently in a heavy-bottomed saucepan. After a few minutes, when the mixture is hot and thick, remove from heat. Spread in a baking pan and let it cool.

The procedure:

Preheat oven to 425°.

Grease and lightly flour a jelly roll pan.
Roll the chilled dough ⅛" thick.

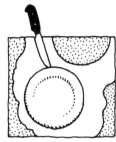

1. Using a 6" saucer as a guide, cut out two circles. Chill them. Reroll the scraps and cut another. Chill it. Reroll the final scraps into the best ⅛" circle you can manage.

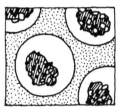

2. Divide the filling into four even glops. Put one glop slightly off center on each circle, taking care to keep it back from the edge; if the filling squishes out between the seam, it won't seal properly.

3. Lightly wet the outer rim of each circle; I use a pastry brush but fingers will do. Fold half the dough over the filled half.

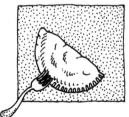

4. Press the seam gently with your fingers, then crimp each with the tines of a fork. Place on a baking pan. Brush each with a little maple syrup. Bake about 25 minutes, until light golden on top. (Chill them if not baking immediately.)

Golden Cornmeal Cake

This is great coffee cake for special occasions or a Saturday brunch. I love thick slices of this with a mug of steaming coffee. You might want to add some chopped walnuts or pecans.

2 sticks soft butter
1 cup maple syrup, room temp.
3 eggs, room temp.
2 teaspoons vanilla
grated zest of 1 orange
1¼ cups unbleached flour
3/4 cups cornmeal
1 tablespoon baking powder
½ teaspoon salt
1½ cups grated coconut
3/4 cup sour cream
1 cup raisins

Preheat oven to 350°.

With an electric mixer, cream the butter. Slowly drizzle in the syrup, beating all the while, and then the eggs (one at a time) and vanilla and orange zest.

Sift together flour, cornmeal, baking powder and salt. Toss in the grated coconut. Add the dry ingredients alternately to the creamed mix with the sour cream, in two or three shots, whisking well to blend. Don't overmix. Mix in raisins. Turn into a buttered tube pan. Bake for 50-60 minutes, until a tester emerges clean. Cool before slicing.

Minnesota Kate's Cosmic Carrot Cake

Once you've tried this, you'll never try another.

4 eggs
1 cup maple syrup
1 1/4 cups oil (nothing assertive)
1/2 cup sour cream
1 tablespoon lemon juice
1 teaspoon each: vanilla & almond extract
1 cup each: whole wheat & unbleached flour
1 1/2 cups finely ground almonds
1/2 teaspoon salt
1 tablespoon baking powder
1 teaspoon each: cinnamon & allspice
grated zest of 1 orange
2 cups grated carrots
1 cup raisins

Preheat oven to 350°.

With an electric mixer, beat the eggs on high speed for a minute. Add next 5 ingredients and continue to beat another minute. Sift the flours. Toss in the almonds, salt, baking powder, spices and orange zest. Make a well in the dry mix, then add the liquid all at once. Mix until smooth — just briefly and don't overmix. Fold in the carrots and raisins. Turn into a buttered 9" x 13" baking pan. Bake for 35-40 minutes, until a toothpick or tester emerges clean.
Frost when cool.

Cosmic Frosting

12 oz. soft cream cheese
2/3 cup maple syrup, room temp.

1 teaspoon vanilla
1 teaspoon grated lemon rind
(optional)

Beat the cream cheese with an electric mixer, drizzling in the maple syrup and vanilla. Mix until lump-less, adding the lemon rind if you like. Ice the cake when it has cooled.

33

Wheat Germ Applesauce Muffins

A hearty, wholesome muffin that stays moist. Serve these for an after-school snack, with a glass of apple cider.

> 1 egg
> 1 cup applesauce
> 3/4 cup maple syrup
> 1/4 cup melted butter
> 2 cups unbleached flour
> 1/2 cup wheat germ
> 2 teaspoons baking powder
> 1/2 teaspoon baking soda
> 1/2 teaspoon salt
> 1 cup raisins

Preheat oven to 375°.

Beat the egg, applesauce, maple syrup and melted butter. In a separate bowl, toss together the remaining ingredients. Make a well in the center and pour in the liquid. Stir gently, just until everything is wet. Spoon the batter into a dozen greased muffin tins. Bake about 20 or 25 minutes.

Zucchini Bread
(with Chinese influences)

This is very pretty if you use yellow summer squash in place of the green zucchini.

3 eggs
1 cup maple syrup
1/2 cup light vegetable oil
2 teaspoons vanilla
2 cups grated zukes or
   summer squash
1 1/4 cup whole wheat flour

1 1/4 cup unbleached flour
2 1/2 teaspoons baking powder
1/2 teaspoon salt
1/4 cup sesame seeds
2 teaspoons dried ginger
   or 1 tablespoon minced
   candied ginger

Preheat oven to 350°.

Beat the eggs with an electric mixer till frothy, about 2 minutes. Add the maple syrup, oil and vanilla while you continue to beat. Stir in the squash.

In a separate bowl, toss together the remaining ingredients. Add this about a cup at a time to the liquid, stirring only to blend after each addition. Don't mix once the dry ingredients are no longer visible.

Pour into a large, buttered loaf pan. Bake about 1 hour, until a tester emerges clean from the center.

Sour Cream Tea Bread

A delicate, yeasted loaf. There's enough dough here for two loaves, but instead why not chill half the dough and make the Cinnamon Sticky Buns on the next page?

> 1 tablespoon dry yeast
> 1 cup warm water (about 110°)
> 2 cups sour cream
> 2/3 cup maple syrup
> 2 egg yolks
> 2 teaspoons salt
> 1/2 teaspoon baking soda
> 2 cups whole wheat flour
> 4 1/2 - 5 cups unbleached flour

Dissolve the yeast in the warm water. Blend in the sour cream, maple syrup, egg yolks, salt and baking soda.

Stir in the whole wheat flour. Beat vigorously for a minute. Cover and let rest for 15 minutes.

Beat in the remaining unbleached flour, 1 cup at a time, stirring thoroughly after each addition. When the dough can no longer be stirred, begin to knead gently in the bowl. Not too hard— this is a bit fragile.

When the dough has firmed up some, turn out onto a floured surface and knead for about 10 minutes, adding more flour to the kneading surface if the dough becomes sticky. Place dough in an oiled bowl, cover and let rise until doubled.

Lightly punch the dough down, knead briefly and divide in half. Shape into loaves (or refrigerate half for the Cinnamon Sticky Buns). Use a standard 8" x 4" loaf pan. Cover and let rise until doubled.

Bake in a preheated 375° oven for about 45 minutes. Brush top crusts with butter when they emerge.

Cinnamon Sticky Buns

Better than any bakery version. To make these you'll need half the dough, refrigerated, from the previous Sour Cream Tea Bread recipe.

> 1/2 cup softened butter
> 1/2 cup maple syrup, room temp.

Cream the butter with an electric mixer. Drizzle in the maple syrup as you beat. Spread this creamed mixture on the bottom and sides of a generous 9" x 13" baking pan. Glass is good but I use my enameled cast-iron lasagna pan.

To prepare the dough:

Roll the chilled dough into a reasonable 13" x 13" square. Pull those corners out and get it as square as you can. Combine in a saucepan:

> 2 tablespoons butter
> 2 tablespoons maple syrup

Heat gently, and as soon as the butter melts spread this evenly over the surface. Then sprinkle on evenly:

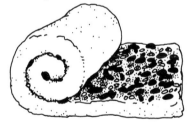

> 1 tablespoon sugar
> 1 tablepoon cinnamon
> 3/4 cup chopped walnuts or pecans
> 3/4 cup raisins

Roll the dough up like a carpet. With a sharp, serrated knife, cut off slices 1" thick — no more. Should end up with about 12. Place these side by side in the pan — 3 across, 4 down. Space them evenly, hopefully with some room between them. Let rise until swollen, but not quite doubled. Bake in a preheated 375° oven for about 25 minutes. Invert onto a baking sheet. Pour the coffee.

Better-Than-The-Monks' Fruitcake

I once wrote an article on mail-order fruitcakes, and in the process I sampled maybe a dozen or more from assorted monasteries, bakeries and other entrepreneurs. Some were very good, some were awful, but the best by far, when all the tasting was said and done, was the following homemade one I've been making for years.

One or two days ahead:

> 12 cups assorted dried fruit (raisins, dates, prunes, dried apples, etc.
> 8 cups assorted nuts (walnuts, pecans, etc. but no Grape-Nuts or peanuts)
> 2 tablespoons finely grated lemon or orange rind
> 4 teaspoons spices (cinnamon, cloves, nutmeg are good)
> 2 cups maple syrup
> 2 cups spirits (rum, brandy or wine; fruit juice for abstainers)

Cut or break the fruit and nuts into edible-size chunks. Place in a large bowl with remaining ingredients. Stir well, about every 8 hours, prior to the baking day. Keep tightly covered, out of mouse range.

Continue next page....

For the cake (baking day)

    2 cups soft butter (unsalted)
    2 cups light brown sugar
    8 large eggs, room temp.
    1 tablespoon vanilla
    4 cups sifted, all-purpose flour
        (may be part whole wheat)
    2 teaspoons salt
    2 teaspoons baking powder

Preheat the oven to 275°.

Cream the butter with an electric mixer. Add the brown sugar and continue to beat until fluffy. Add the eggs, one at a time, mixing well after each addition. Briefly beat in vanilla.

Toss together flour, salt and powder. Beat into the creamed mixture, a cup at a time, mixing until smooth after each addition. Combine batter with fruit and nut mix — use your hands, because that's the only way to do a really thorough job. Fill greased, wax-paper-lined pans approximately 3/4 full. Large cakes will take up to 3 hours to bake; small ones about an hour. Check with a tester.

Remove cakes to a wire rack. While cakes are still barely warm, de-pan and peel off the waxed paper. Brush with spirits. After 12 hours wrap the cakes in muslin, brush with more spirits and store in plastic bags. Every few days, re-apply the spirits.

These can be eaten right away, or stored for months in a cool, airtight environment.

Woodstock Inn Frozen Maple Soufflé

A house specialty from Vermont's elegant Woodstock Inn, in the heart of maple syrup country. I offer you two versions.

Their version:

5 egg whites
2/3 cup sugar
1 pint whipping cream
1/4 cup maple syrup
2 egg yolks

Beat the egg whites, adding 1 tablespoon of the sugar when slightly foamy. Beat until stiff, adding remainder of the sugar gradually.

Whip the cream, drizzling in the maple syrup and egg yolks when partially stiff. Beat until stiff. Fold into egg whites. Spoon into goblets or custard cups and freeze. (For better consistency, stir in a tablespoon of vanilla ice cream before freezing.) Top with whipped cream and sprinkle with walnuts. Pour additional syrup over.

My version of their version:

Omit the sugar. When cream is partially stiff, drizzle in slowly 1/2 cup maple syrup. Beat until stiff, adding egg yolks as well. Fold together with egg whites. Freeze and serve as above.

Maple Graham Crackers

I've always considered a bowl of crushed graham crackers doused with light cream one of life's great comfort foods. This is how I make them.

> 1½ cups whole wheat flour
> 1½ cups unbleached flour
> 1 teaspoon baking powder
> ½ teaspoon salt
> ½ cup maple syrup
> ⅓ cup melted butter
> 1 egg

Preheat oven to 375°.

Combine the dry ingredients and toss together with your hands. In a separate bowl, lightly beat remaining ingredients.

Make a well in the dry ingredients, then add the liquids. Work with your hands until the dough coheres. Dust lightly with flour, then roll into a rectangle ⅛" thick. The dough will appear to stick, but don't worry. Cut into squares or rectangles and pierce each with a fork 3 or 4 times. Transfer to an ungreased baking sheet using a spatula or baker's scraper. Bake approximately 15 minutes.

Indian Pudding

I've read that Durgin Park in Boston serves the best Indian pudding in the country. I've had theirs. This is better.

5 cups milk
2/3 cup cornmeal
1/2 teaspoon salt
1/3 cup molasses
2/3 cup maple syrup
4 tablespoons butter
1 teaspoon each, ginger & cinnamon
1 cup raisins or chopped dates
   (optional)

Preheat oven to 300°.

In a large saucepan, cautiously heat milk. Sprinkle on the cornmeal, whisking thoroughly. Keep the heat medium high and continue to stir for about 10 minutes, or until the mixture begins to thicken. Lower heat, add remaining ingredients and cook for another couple of minutes. Keep stirring. Pour into a buttered 9" x 13" baking dish and bake for 2-3 hours. Serve warm with whipped cream or ice cream. About 8 servings.

Cinnamon-Nut Swirl (Ice Cream)

This is your basic maple ice cream with a bit of fantasy added. Serve with pie or cakes. It's tremendous.

> 1 cup light cream
> ⅓ cup sugar
> ⅔ cup maple syrup
> 2 teaspoons vanilla

Gently heat the cream, sugar and maple syrup in a heavy saucepan. Stir for several minutes, just until the sugar is dissolved. Remove from heat and stir in vanilla. Pour into a shallow casserole and chill in the fridge until very cold.

> 1 cup light cream
> 1½ cups heavy cream
> ½ cup milk

After the first mixture has chilled, add that and the above three ingredients to the freezing can of an ice cream machine. Process according to the manufacturer's directions. While one person cranks, another should make up the

Cinnamon-Nut Swirl Stuff

> ½ cup maple syrup
> 1 cup chopped nuts of your choice
> ½ teaspoon cinnamon

Bring maple syrup to a boil in a small, heavy saucepan. Boil for exactly two minutes. Pour into a bowl, add nuts and cinnamon. Stir vigorously. When mixture is thick and gooey, spread on a pan and refrigerate. Add to the ice cream a couple of minutes before you stop cranking. (Be sure the nuts are not hot!)

Baked Custard

I love baked cup custard with a dollop of whipped cream. One of the simplest desserts I know. Make this early in the day so it has plenty of time to chill for a dinner dessert or after-school snack.

4 eggs
1/2 cup maple syrup
1 teaspoon vanilla
1/4 teaspoon salt
3 cups milk, heated just
   to the boiling point

Preheat oven to 350°

With a whisk, beat together the eggs, syrup, vanilla and salt. Slowly whisk in the hot milk. Ladle into custard cups, filling each to within a quarter inch of the top rim. Place cups in a large baking pan and pour hot water into the pan until it comes about halfway up the cups. Bake 45 minutes to an hour. I take the custard out just before it seems completely done because the accumulated heat finishes it to a perfect texture. Chill thoroughly before serving. This recipe makes enough for 8 good-sized custard cups.

Blueberry Grunt

This grunt is like a buckle, which is like a cobbler. The apples go well with the berries, but if you prefer just use all berries.

2 cups blueberries
1 cup apples, peeled, cored and chopped
1/3 cup maple syrup
1/2 teaspoon each : cinnamon and allspice
grated rind of 1 lemon

Combine above in saucepan. Heat gently. Pour into a buttered 8" x 8" pan.

For the top: 1 cup flour
1 1/2 teaspoons baking powder
1/4 teaspoon salt
3 tablespoons butter
2 tablespoons each : maple syrup and milk

Preheat oven to 400°

Sift the dry ingredients. Cut the butter into the dry until the pieces are about the size of small peas. Blend syrup and milk then add to the flour, tossing with a fork or hands. The dough should be niether too wet nor too dry. Dust dough with flour then roll into a square 8"x 8". Lay on top of fruit mixture and bake about 20 minutes. 6-9 servings.

A Gallon of Granola

Every Christmas I prepare large batches of this recipe for my friends and family. Makes a great stocking stuffer.

8 cups rolled oats
2 cups coarsely chopped nuts
   (cashews, pecans, almonds, or peanuts)
2 cups sunflower seeds
1 cup sesame seeds
1 cup coconut
1 teaspoon salt
3/4 cup maple syrup
3/4 cup light oil (not olive or
   anything strong)
2 cups chopped, dried fruit
   (raisins, currants, dates are good)

Preheat oven to 300°.

In a large mixing bowl, toss together the first six (dry) ingredients. Warm maple syrup and oil together in a saucepan. Pour over the dry. Stir with a wooden spoon then roll up your sleeves and work the mixture with your hands until everything is wet. Spread on baking sheets — no more than about ½" thick — and roast for 30-40 minutes, stirring occasionally, until golden. When the granola has cooled, stir in the dried fruit. Store in jars or plastic bags.

Variations: Instead of all oats use other grain flakes. Some of the seeds could be replaced by bran or wheat germ.

Also by Ken Haedrich

There's probably no more far-out thing you can do for anybody than to offer them a gift of your own wholesome, homemade bread. Baking bread is easier than you might think. It slows you down, puts you in a meditative state —even if you don't believe in meditation. And using whole grains makes the whole experience just that much more soul-satisfying.

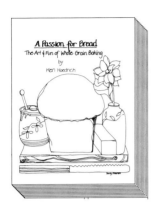

A Passion for Bread offers you a veritable cornucopia of healthy breads, from easy muffins to exotica like Swedish Limpa, and Curried Potato Paranthas. To name a few more:

Yeasted Breads: Anadama, Banana Buckwheat Tea Bread, Braided Egg Loaf, Breadsticks, Basic Whole Wheat, Cuban Bread, Parker House Rolls, Sourdough, Toasted Cornmeal Loaf, Yogurt Rye, Sesame Pumpernickle, Bagels, Pita, Bulghur Bread, Barley-Corn Bread, Kasha Millet-meal Bread, Peasant Black Bread.

Unyeasted Breads and Flat Breads: Unyeasted Pumpernickle, Unyeasted Corn and Oat Bread, Onion Flat Bread, Tortillas, Chapatti, Puri.

Quick Breads and Pancakes: New England Corn Cakes, Sour Rye Cakes, Buttermilk Bran Muffins, Basic Muffins with lots of variations, Buckwheat Griddle Cakes, Sour Cream Carob Cakes, Popovers, Cream Scones, Irish Soda Bread, Custard Skillet Bread and more

So, be you a seasoned baker, part-time gourmet, or even if you don't know a bread board from a skate board, you'll want to own (or give) a copy of **A Passion for Bread**. Other features include:

- Easy, illustrated instructions for working with whole grains. Tips on kneading, rising, mixing and baking.

- Helpful observations about the "Tools of the Trade".

- The straight skinny on ingredients. Covers the basics — grains, fats, sweeteners and leavenings.

See order form on the next page.

American Impressions Book Co.
Box 101
Rumney, NH 03266

Dear Friends,
   Please send _____ autographed copy/ies of
The Maple Syrup Baking and Dessert Cookbook
to me/my friend. I enclose $4.50 for each book ordered,
plus $1.00 postage and handling. (50¢ extra for each
additional book ordered.)

Name _____

Address _____

_____

Send a gift card signed _____

American Impressions Book Co.
Box 101
Rumney, NH 03266

Dear Friends,
   Please send _____ autographed copy/ies of
A Passion for Bread : The Art & Fun of Whole Grain Baking
to me/my friend. I enclose $4.50 for each book ordered,
plus $1.00 postage and handling. (50¢ for each extra
additional book ordered.)

Name _____

Address _____

_____

Send a gift card signed _____

Do you have a friend who'd like to receive some free recipes and
literature about our books? Do you know of a store that might
like to carry them? If so, could you please fill in their address
below and we'll send the information along. Thank you.

Name _____

Address _____

_____